While the Sun Shines

Making Hay in Vermont 1789-1990

D1298413

While the Sun Shines

Making Hay in Vermont 1789-1990

by Allen R. Yale, Jr.

Vermont Historical Society
Montpelier, Vermont

Distributed by University Press of New England
Hanover and London

Library of Congress Cataloging-in-Publication Data

Yale, Allen R., 1942-
    While the sun shines : making hay in Vermont, 1789-1990 / Allen R. Yale, Jr.
      p.   cm.
    Includes bibliographical references.
    ISBN 0-934720-35-5
    1. Hay--Vermont--History.   I. Title.
SB198.Y35   1991
633.2'009743--dc20   91-26434
                                                  CIP

ISBN 0-934720-35-5

EDITOR: Susan Bartlett Weber

Designed by The Laughing Bear Associates, Inc.
Printed by Northlight Studio Press
Typeset in Garamond by Accura Type & Design

Contents

Preface

In 1857 Hinton Rowan Helper, a southerner, wrote a book, *The Impending Crisis of the South*, to persuade the South of the economic impracticality of slavery. In it he argued that the value of the hay crop in the North exceeded that of King Cotton.[1] Yet in the history of American agriculture hay has been overshadowed by crops such as wheat and cotton. Since people do not consume hay directly, it is "invisible" in the lives of most Americans. Even farmers rarely view hay as a cash crop; it is eaten by livestock on the same farm where it is harvested, and usually is not assigned a specific monetary value. Yet hay, as a major livestock food, demands much time and effort from the farmers who raise the cattle, sheep, or horses that have been a major part of agriculture in Vermont during the past two hundred years.

This study examines the experiences of Vermont farmers during haying season at four distinct technological stages in the past two centuries. By chronicling the evolution of haying technology, it captures something of the interaction of people and their tools as labor scarcity fostered technological change.

The engine that drove the changes in agricultural technology was the Industrial Revolution. Many of the changes in this technology are directly related to developments in the industrial sector: in metallurgy, the development of mechanical power, the mass manufacture of iron implements, and the introduction of the tractor.

The Industrial Revolution also affected agriculture by enticing rural laborers to the cities. While farm mechanization relieved some of the hard work and tedium of farming, industrial wages rose and hours decreased more rapidly than wages and hours on the farm. Many a farm boy was drawn to the perceived excitement, ease, and wealth offered by the city. At the same time the growth of industrial cities greatly increased the demand for agricultural commodities. This demand stimulated a proportionally smaller farm population to greatly expand productivity. The shortage of farm labor and the increased demand for agricultural commodities conspired to make expensive labor-saving machinery the best economic choice for a farmer who wished to succeed. This decision to replace labor with machines also made it possible for women and children to do some of the work previously done by men.

This study traces the transition to mechanization and increased productivity that occurred on Vermont farms during the nineteenth and twentieth centuries. Marshall Castle, haying in Essex, Vermont, in the early 1830s, used methods that had changed little for centuries. The hay was cut with a scythe, raked by hand, tedded, cocked, tumbled, loaded and unloaded with a pitchfork. Oxen were used only to pull the cart that transported the hay. This was truly a period of manual labor.

By the mid-nineteenth century the horse became the chief supplier of agricultural power. For approximately a century, the transitional period between the age of manpower and the present age of machine power, horse power dominated. By 1882, when Charles Hinman of Derby was haying, horse-drawn machinery was common. Hay was mowed, tedded, raked, and transported with horses, but loading and unloading were still done by hand. Fifty years later the same farm, under the management of Wellman Rowell, had begun to use tractors, but Rowell still loaded and unloaded hay in ways that had been developed for horse power.

By the 1980s the horse as a source of agricultural power was gone from the fields. The tractor, with a minor assist from the electric motor, now dominated every aspect of haying; haybines, tedders, rakes, and balers were all driven by tractor power. In some cases the farmer never touched the hay until it was time to feed it out. Don Kilborn's operation illustrates one of the permutations of this modern haying technology.

Manuscript sources and the oral histories I recorded helped greatly to enrich the history of these particular farms. Marshall Castle had kept a diary from 1830 to 1834, which included a brief entry for each day. In 1882 Marshall Carpenter, the owner of the farm hayed by Charles Hinman, sent a letter detailing conditions on the farm to his grandchildren who had gone West the previous summer. (See appendix.) Wellman Rowell's widow and son were willing to be interviewed, as was a subsequent owner of the Carpenter farm, Stanley Wilson. Don Kilborn, Sr., and his son, Don, Jr., from a neighboring farm, shared their two-generation perspective. I presently live on the same farm that Carpenter, Hinman, Rowell, and Wilson hayed. For several years, using a technology that was fifteen to twenty years old, I harvested ten to twelve tons of hay a year from this land.

Since I was using limited material about specific individuals, some interpolation from the general to the particular was necessary. Where diaries or letters were silent, I consulted contemporary equipment manuals and agricultural literature to aid in my reconstruction.

This project began as a masters thesis at the University of Vermont. I am indebted to the faculty of its history department. A special thanks goes to Dr. Samuel B. Hand, my thesis advisor. The staff of the Wilbur Collection at the Bailey/Howe Library, University of Vermont, provided valuable assistance.

Most important were those Vermont farm folk who were willing to share their knowledge so that a part of Vermont's rural past could be preserved. They include Elaine Anderson of Craftsbury; Silas Houghton, who grew up in Red Village, Lyndonville; Donald Kilborn, Sr., Donald Kilborn, Jr., Douglas Nelson, Ethel Rowell, Kenneth Rowell, and Stanley Wilson, all of Derby.

I would like to thank Sam Hand, James Hayford, Susan Bartlett Weber, and my wife Kathleen for editing the many versions of this manuscript.

Want of Good Hay

Seth Hubbell 1789

S eth Hubbell trudged through the deep drifts, a heavy
bundle of hay on his back. He had almost completed
the five miles from Cambridge, Vermont, to Johnson and
his sick ox. That February, 1789, while Seth was moving
his family from Connecticut to a new home in Wolcott,
one of his oxen had taken sick. It struggled on for eighty
miles until at Johnson a Thomas Connel agreed to care for
it. Seth negotiated with a man in Cambridge for a little hay,
and for the past ten days had made the trip there and back,
on snowshoes, to fetch it. Despite this extraordinary effort,
Seth lost his valuable ox.[1]

During the summer of 1789 Seth Hubbell expanded a
clearing in Wolcott's virgin forest to make a farm for his
family. There was little or no vegetation in the shade of the
forest that covered the hills. After giving his other ox as pay-
ment for his land, Seth was left with a single cow. During
the summer it lived off browse: wild grass, leaves, twigs,
ferns, and sedge. The cow ate the leaves of the hardwood
trees that Seth had felled and the sprouts from the stumps
of trees he cut the previous year when he had made his
first trip to stake out his land. But as fall came the leaves of
the hardwoods fell and before long the ground was covered with snow. The following winter there was little to
feed the cow and she starved to death.[2]

When the first settlers began to clear forest-covered Vermont, only an occasional beaver meadow, ledge, burned-over area, or Indian field interrupted the forest canopy. The vegetation in these few openings offered little nutrition for domesticated livestock. Earlier settlers in southern New England had already reported the deficiencies of native American grasses. Thomas Hutchinson's *History of Massachusetts* noted that the "hay we have here . . . is inferior in goodness to our reed and sedge in England, for it is so devoid of nutritive virtue, that our beasts grow lousy with feeding upon it." Indeed, "the colonials were often under necessity of slaughtering their livestock to keep them from starvation." Recognizing this impediment to settlement of the wilderness, New Hampshire's Gov. Benning Wentworth required in many grants that each grantee stock five acres with English grass within three years.[3]

In due time, through prodigious effort, the settlers of the New Hampshire Grants, later known as Vermont, conquered the forest. In less than one hundred years these settlers had, by farming and logging, dramatically changed the face of the land. By 1850, three-quarters of Vermont had been cleared and much of it abounded in timothy, clover, and other English grasses.

Once this battle had been won, another began: the battle to harvest and store enough hay to feed livestock through the six-month winter when, in Vermont and other northern states, most vegetation is dormant and snow-covered. For most of its history, Vermont's agriculture concentrated on animal husbandry, and maintaining sheep, cattle, and horses requires substantial quantities of hay. To harvest this hay in the brief summer season meant tremendous amounts of work for the farmer and his family. The naturalist John Burroughs wrote vividly of this challenge from his own farm in neighboring New York in 1886.

3.

Haying is the period of "storm and stress" in the farmer's year. To get the hay in, in good condition, and before the grass gets too ripe, is a great matter. All the energies and resources of the farm are bent to this purpose. It is a thirty or forty days' war, in which the farmer and his "hands" are pitted against the heat and rain and the legions of timothy and clover.[4]

Putting added pressure on the farmer is the fact that the nutritive value of grass is highest at one point in its development, just prior to blossoming. Moreover, once the grass is cut microorganisms break down the plant fibers, diminishing the nutrients until the hay is dried to about twenty-five percent moisture content and nutrients become fixed. For maximum nutrition a farmer must cut the hay when it reaches its optimum stage and then dry it as quickly as possible.

Once dried, the hay must then be kept dry. The plentiful rainfall and moderate temperatures that provide the northeastern United States with such an excellent climate for growing grasses are, unfortunately, detrimental during haying. Rain is the enemy of good hay and cool weather prolongs the drying process, increasing the time that the hay is exposed to the risk of rain.

Over the past two hundred years the steps in making hay in Vermont have remained fairly constant. The grass is cut to separate the stalk from the moisture-supplying roots, then exposed to sun and wind, and perhaps turned or fluffed up to hurry the drying. Once dry, the hay is gathered, transported to shelter, and "put up." The technology of haymaking, however, has changed dramatically. Technological innovations have speeded the haymaking process, increased production, made the work less arduous, and enabled fewer workers to do more.

Scythe and Oxen
Marshall Castle 1831

By 1831 when Marshall Castle was farming the bottom-land along the Brown River near Essex Center, most Vermonters were no longer living the frontier experience of Seth Hubbell. Vermont had become a state of agricultural villages and well-ordered farmsteads. Castle, age fifty-one, lived with his second wife, Lindamira, age thirty-five; their five-year-old son, Hawley; and Pearl, the twenty-three-year-old son by Marshall's first wife.[1] The Castles raised hay, wheat, oats, rye, apples, peas, potatoes, flax, corn, cattle, hogs, sheep, and probably poultry. Mr. Castle's diary also records that he sold or bartered butter and wool.[2]

Springtime at the Castles was filled with mending fences, carting manure from the barnyard to the field, sowing wheat and oats, planting corn and potatoes, shearing sheep, and hoeing corn and potatoes. Then, as the rush of spring chores subsided, Marshall prepared for haying. On Saturday, June 25, 1831, he traveled to Underhill to hire George Bicknal for the haying season. Marshall's diary indicates that George was paid fifty cents a day plus board.[3]

June 27 Marshall and Pearl spent "fixing for haying." A major task was to place the hayrack on the two-wheeled ox-cart.[4] Then they went to the toolroom to prepare the haying tools. First, they took the scythes down from their pegs on the wall. Pearl turned the grindstone, while his father sharpened the scythe blades. Then Marshall checked the condition of the hay rakes. A couple of teeth were broken on one. Locating a piece of seasoned ash in a corner of the toolroom, he sawed off a six-inch section. At the chopping block he split several tooth blanks with a hatchet. With his knife Marshall whittled three of the blanks into teeth. After knocking out the broken stubs with a punch and mallet, he tapped these new teeth into place. Rummaging in the tool chest, he found the whetstones for sharpening the scythes in the field. Marshall asked Pearl to gather up the wooden pitchforks, which they had been using all winter in the stable and hayloft.

Bull rake for raking scatterings.

Early on the morning of June 30 Marshall and Pearl began haying.[5] The next day, while Pearl stayed to rake the hay that they had mowed the day before, Marshall made a trip to Burlington where he bought "two mow sythes [*sic*]."

Haying season is a period of several weeks in which the same two- or three-day process is repeated over and over. On July 10 Marshall asked Mr. Gates, his neighbor, to help him the next day; other neighbors, John Sinclair and Dr. Shattuck, joined them from July 12 to 14.

The sun rises at about 4:30 A.M. in mid-July, but on the morning of the twelfth the hayers were up even earlier. In the pre-dawn light the men washed, dressed, and did the morning chores. The sun was almost visible when Marshall, Pearl, and hired hand George Bicknal stepped out into the yard. They had just begun to whet their blades when their neighbors, scythes on shoulders, came up the road. After greeting one another, the six men headed down to the field that they wanted to mow that morning.

The early morning air felt cool as the rising sun's rays filtered through the haze that lifted from the field, but the men knew that their toil and the warming of the sun would soon make them sweat. Marshall slid open the bars of the gate, and two of the men trimmed grass alongside the road, as if testing the sharpness of their blades. Inside the fence, in the early morning stillness, the weight of the dew bent the timothy's seedheads, shaped like tiny cattails, in delicate arcs. The prospect of having to cut acres of waist-high grass may cause a single mower to lose heart, but the friendly competitiveness of the several scythemen would ease and quicken the job.

The stillness was broken by the ringing of whetstones as each man whetted his blade until his scythe was brought to razor-sharp keenness. For a moment the mowers hesitated before plunging into the sea of grass. Marshall led off, heading along the outside of the field in a clockwise direction, his scythe making apparently effortless arcs to the left, felling legions of grass stalks in its path. As he swung the scythe back, he moved his left foot forward and then his right, advancing about a foot each time. After Marshall had mowed about ten feet, the next man started mowing to the right of Marshall's swath, so that his cut grass landed in an even row on the ground, partially in the swath cleared by Marshall and partially in his own. In un-spoken agreement, each of the other men started in his own turn. Soon all six were mowing in a smooth, synchro-nized rhythm.[6]

A good mower is proud of his skill. He tries to keep his scythe blade parallel to the ground so that he leaves no ridge at the edge of his swath. When the hay is raked away it is a great embarrassment if small patches of uncut grass are left standing.

Although the heavy dew soaked the men's shoes, they preferred to mow in early morning because the grass cut more easily then. Dew gave it greater weight and inertia so that it cut cleanly.[7] At the end of the field they paused to wipe the sweat from their brows and take a pull at the water jug. They whetted their blades for the next pass.

Agricultural historian Jared Van Wagenen described a similar scene in nineteenth-century New York:

> Always they laughed and gossiped and chaffed a little. Then the man whose turn it was to lead struck three smart taps with his stone upon his scythe, a sound that was both a signal and a challenge, and they were off. If someone lagged in his stroke, the fellow literally at his heels cried out the jocular warning, "Get out of my way or I'll cut your legs off."[8]

Around and around the field went the mowers. The six men dropped close to fifty feet of grass with each pass.[9] The uncut section in the center of the field, which had appeared so intimidating when they began, diminished ap-preciably. With each circling, the remaining island of grass narrowed and shortened by almost a hundred feet.

About 6:30 A.M. it was time for breakfast. Hanging their scythes in the tree beside the gate, the men trooped to the farmhouse. After washing at the pump, they seated themselves around the kitchen table. Awaiting them were platters of corn griddlecakes called corn dodger, bowls of boiled potatoes, salt pork in cream gravy, fresh-fried doughnuts, and mugs of steaming tea.[10] Heaping their plates with food, the men settled down to eating. There was no talking except for an occasional request for more food, and the men cleaned their plates in short order. After the luxury of a few moments to swallow their tea, the men left with a scraping of chairs and some muffled "thank you, ma'ams."

Once outside they picked up the pitchforks, which they would need later in the morning. Once more in the hayfield, the men whetted their scythes. Soon Marshall signalled with three taps on his blade, and the mowing started again.

At about nine Marshall asked Pearl and George to ted the new-mown hay. They hung their scythes in a nearby tree, picked up pitchforks, and spread the hay out evenly, shaking apart every clump, and fluffing it up to encourage air circulation. Starting at the same place where they had begun to mow, each man picked up successive forkfuls and, with a shake of the pitchfork, tossed one toward a spot of bare ground. Any tangle of wet hay was shaken vigorously. While these two tedded the new-mown hay, the others tedded what they had mown two days before and later piled in small mounds, or cocks, to protect it from the anticipated heavy dew.[11]

At midday Lindamira and her sister, Eliza, arrived with hampers of food and a small keg of switchel, a favorite thirst-quencher, made of water, syrup, vinegar, and ground ginger. The haymakers finished a last turn of the field and, hungry and tired, hurried to the maple tree under whose shade the women had spread dinner. The men headed first for the drink to slake their thirst. Then they attacked the mounds of food. After dinner the hayers stretched out on the ground for a two-hour nap.

Marshall woke first and roused the others. While they finished tedding, Marshall checked the field that they had mown two days before and tedded that morning. Judging that the hay was dry, Marshall sent Pearl to the farmyard to bring down the haycart and oxen. Meanwhile, he and the four other men walked over to the field. Three of them raked the hay into windrows while two tumbled.

A tumble is a forkful of hay small enough to pitch easily onto the haycart. To make one, you place the hayfork, tines up, under the windrow about one foot from the end, lift it, and fold it over upon itself. About three feet down the windrow lift another forkful and lay it onto the previous fold. This forms a three-layered bundle about two feet wide and two feet high. Sometimes a little downward pressure of fork or foot is necessary to keep the tumble from unfolding.[12]

George started by making four tumbles from each windrow. Beginning at the edge of the field, he forked the first tumble away from the edge. He forked the next tumble toward the outside of the field so that it ended up near the first one. He forked the third tumble toward the center of the field and left it six or eight feet from the second. Then he forked the fourth tumble toward the third. Thus there were two pairs of tumbles with a "road" between the pairs through which the haycart would pass.

Up in the farmyard Pearl came out of the barn with the ox yoke over one shoulder, the gad, or switch, in his hand, and two oxbows over his arm. He leaned the yoke against the barnyard fence and hung the bows on the top rail. Pearl then drove the two oxen, Buck and Bright, to the fence where they stood side by side calmly chewing their cuds. Lifting the yoke, he placed it across the oxen's necks. Next he hung one of the bows temporarily on Buck's left horn, placed the other under the ox's neck, and brought it up through the two holes in the yoke. When the bow was fully in place two small square holes appeared just above where it came through the yoke. In these holes Pearl inserted the bow keys, which prevented the bow from coming out. Retrieving the other bow from Buck's horn, Pearl repeated the process with Bright.[13]

At voice command the second ox moves forward for yoking.

Finally, Pearl slid back the bars of the gate and drove the oxen to the haycart. He backed them on either side of the cart pole, then, ducking between them, raised the pole and attached it to the ring of the yoke.

When Pearl arrived in the field with the haycart, George and Dr. Shattuck left their tumbling to help him load hay. Dr. Shattuck stood on the cart to make the load, while Pearl and George thrust their pitchforks into successive tumbles and pitched them onto the hayrack. Dr. Shattuck carefully distributed it on the cart. An attentively made load will hold together despite the cart's jouncing and yet be easy to unload back at the barn.

A "giddap" from Dr. Shattuck urged the oxen slowly forward, while a "whoa" stopped them; thus his hands were free to make the load. When the cart was full, Dr. Shattuck sat down in the middle of the load while Pearl guided

Proper placement of tumbles becomes more important near top.

the oxen toward the barn. He walked by the left side of the oxen, driving them with a "haw, haw" for a left turn or "gee, gee" for a right turn, each command reinforced by a tap of the gad on the opposite shoulder.

Once the haycart stopped inside the barn, Pearl climbed into the haymow, and Dr. Shattuck began to fork the hay from the cart. He tossed it to Pearl who mowed it away, distributing it evenly throughout the mow, making sure that the hay in the corners and ends was kept level with that in the center. Walking on the hay helped to pack it down.

"Back, Buck; back, Bright!" Pearl coaxed the oxen when the cart was empty, and gave each a gentle tap on the nose with the gad. With a series of reassuring "backs" to first one ox and then the other, he slowly guided the cart out of the barn. Both men climbed aboard and with a "gid-dap" returned to the hayfield for another load.

By late afternoon, when they broke off haying to do evening chores, they had gathered nine loads. Still they were not finished. After supper they raked into windrows the hay that had been mowed the day before, then made the windrows into cocks. If the weather continued fair, they could leave the hay for two or three days to dry and then cart it to the barn.

In four days Marshall and his crew hauled thirty-eight loads to the barn. Later in the season, after the mows in the barn were full, they would store the rest of the hay outside in stacks or ricks. Sometimes they built the stack on a stone or wooden platform known as a staddle, or on a layer of ferns, called bracken, placed on the ground to serve as a moisture barrier. To form a stack they made a circle of tumbles with a diameter of about ten feet. Inside the first circle of tumbles they set a smaller circle and so on until the first layer was finished. Subsequent layers were similarly built. After the stack was about four feet high, the diameter of each succeeding layer was decreased; this gave the stack a dome-shaped appearance. Sometimes a thatched roof or staddle roof protected the stack from the weather.[14]

Dome shape protects hay from rain.

Marshall finished haying on July 31 and paid George Bicknall $12.50 for four weeks of work. Six men using hand tools, with no assistance from animal power except the oxen who moved the hay from field to barn, had harvested approximately thirty tons of hay in one month's time.

In the quiet of pre-mechanized farming the long hours of shared work afforded abundant opportunity for banter and gossip and forged strong bonds of neighborliness.

Mower and Dump Rake

Charles Hinman 1882

By 1882, fifty-one years after our summer with Marshall Castle, many changes had occurred in haying technology. Horse-powered implements had relieved some of the hand drudgery, but haying season was only slightly less hectic. Mechanization had been directed towards increasing production with a reduced labor force, but those engaged in haying still found the season long, tedious, and exhausting. Such was the case on the Marshall Carpenter farm in Derby, located one mile west of the village of Derby Center at the end of a road that passed a cluster of mills and artisans' shops powered by the Clyde River in its descent from Salem Pond to Lake Memphremagog.

Over half of the 150-acre Carpenter farm was too steep for anything but woodland and pasture, but about seventy acres were suitable for tillage or mowing meadows. This gently sloping land ran east-west through the center of the farm.

Until now Mr. Carpenter had farmed his land with his son Henry. In the spring of 1882, however, Henry, his wife, and four children left Derby to settle in the Dakota Territory. Unable to run the farm alone, Marshall leased it to Charles Hinman and his family. Mr. Carpenter and his wife Harriet continued to live in a part of the farmhouse, but the daily operation of the farm was now the responsibility of thirty-six-year-old Hinman, his wife Clara, and their three children: Albert, age fourteen, Clarence, age twelve, and Nellie, age ten.[1] The stock consisted of three horses, thirteen milk cows, ten other cattle, thirty-five sheep, five hogs, and thirty-nine chickens. Besides providing meat, milk, eggs, wheat, corn, apples, and vegetables for home consumption, the farm produced butter, wool, maple sugar, and potatoes for market.[2]

Mr. Carpenter remained interested in the operation of the farm. In the year following his son's move he shared his apprehensions about the 1882 hay crop in a letter to Henry and his family:

> The winter was probably the hardest one for the grass crop of any for many years. Our repeated snows, thaws, and bare ground killed almost the whole of the clover of every variety, the Red, Alsike and White all went together. We had no clover on the farm this year except on the hill where we raised oats and rye last year, and that was greatly injured. There is no white clover growing this year, I do not think I have seen a hundred blossoms this year in highway or pasture. The piece of Red Clover that grew North West of the barn last year where we mowed the second crop, and fed it to the cows was clean Herds Grass this year, not a stalk of any kind of clover to be found on it, and so with every piece of grass upon the farm except the first piece spoken of. The spring was very cold and backward, and up to past the middle of June it seemed that our Hay would be a failure.[3]

During the spring plowing, harrowing, and planting, Hinman looked toward the meadows with a sense of discouragement. This farm, which had been reputed to be so fat with grass and clover when he leased it, appeared barren. But, as Carpenter reported to his son's family, "after the weather became warmer grass began to grow and thicken up."[4] Hinman wondered if the grass would be ready to cut by the Fourth of July, the traditional day to start haying.

A few days before the Fourth, Hinman began to check the haying equipment. While the scythe and handrake still played a small part in haying, horse-drawn machines now did most of the mowing, raking, and tedding. As Hinman and his two boys moved the mower, tedder, and dump rake out of the equipment shed, Mr. Carpenter came from the house to watch; he pointed out where the spare section knives and rivets for the mower were stored.

Albert and Clarence turned the grindstone, while Hinman sharpened one mower section (the part that reciprocates to do the cutting). The knives on the other section were worn, so he knocked them off and riveted new ones onto the knifeback. Inserting one section into the mower, Hinman checked to see whether the knife holders were pressing the cutters close enough to the edge of the steel plates in the guards. A couple of knife holders needed adjusting, so he rapped them with a hammer to close the gaps. He then rapped the bottoms of several guards to close the remaining gaps. Finally, he oiled and tested the moving parts of all three machines to be sure they moved freely.

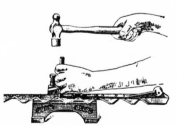

Since in 1882 the Fourth of July fell in the middle of the week, and since it was considered bad luck to start a big job late in the week, Hinman decided to begin haying the following Monday. On Sunday he searched the sky for signs

Top: *Removing worn knife from section.*
Bottom: *Riveting new knife to section.*

of the morrow's weather. The red sunset foretold that the next day would be dry.

Early Monday morning the sunlight streaming through the bedroom window woke Hinman. As he finished dressing, the parlor clock struck five. Albert joined him as he splashed cold water from the outside pump on his hands and face. Together they headed for the barn to milk and tend the stock.

Meanwhile, Clara began to prepare breakfast. With paper and finely-split kindling she soon had the fire burning in the cookstove. At the pitcher pump she filled two kettles and the coffee pot and placed them on the back of the stove. From the pantry she fetched a dozen potatoes, peeled them, set them to boil in one of the kettles, and then woke the two younger children. She sliced some salt pork into her black skillet. Clarence came down and went to the barn to feed and water the horses while Nellie set the table.

In the barn, Clarence's father and brother sat on three-legged milking stools. With each squeeze of their hands a stream of milk shot into the pail. Occasionally Albert would squirt milk into the face of one of the barn kittens, who would then lick the milk from its fur.

As each cow was milked out, the pail of milk was dumped into a milk can. When they were finished with the morning chores, they would carry the milk cans to the dairy room. Later that morning Clara would pour the milk into shallow pans so that the cream would rise.

Shortly after seven everyone sat down to large bowls of oatmeal, followed by the salt pork in milk gravy, boiled potatoes, and platters of muffins and doughnuts. There was milk for the children and coffee for Hinman. After breakfast, the dew still shone on the grass, so Hinman put off the mowing for another hour. Unlike Marshall Castle fifty years earlier, he preferred to wait until the dew had burned off before he started mowing. While waiting he whetted his scythe; he still made it a practice to mow by hand along the road and around trees, bushes, and stone-piles. Once the scythe was sharp, he sent Albert to cut the grass around the gate in the field to be mowed that morning.

Friendly nickers and the stamping of hooves on the hemlock floor greeted Hinman and Clarence as they entered the barn to harness the haying team—Old Sally, the mare, and "Newmare horse," the gelding. Hinman first brought the harness collar up under the gelding's neck and buckled it at the top. From the harness hook on the wall, he took the breeching in his right hand and put it on his right shoulder. Then he took the right hame in his right hand and the left one in his left hand. From the left side of the horse, Hinman threw the right hame over the horse's back, near the collar. Setting the backstraps over the gelding's back, he threw the breeching up on the horse's hip. Going forward, he put the hames into the creases of

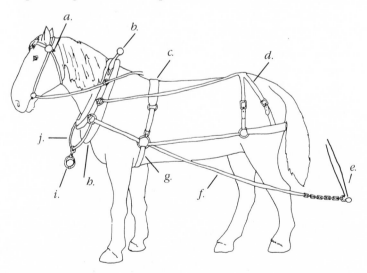

a. throatlatch   b. hames   c. saddle   d. breeching   e. whiffletree
f. traces   g. girth   h. collar   i. neck yoke   j. yoke strap

the collar and tightened them. Then he pulled the breeching down over the horse's hips and lifted its tail out from under the strap. From the side he attached and tightened the belly girth. Finally, removing the halter, Hinman forced the bridle bit into the horse's mouth, fitted the bridle over its head, and buckled the throatlatch.[5]

Hinman fed the outside rein through the top ring of the hames and, after doing the same with the inside rein, he temporarily hooked the inside rein to the outside one, doubled up the reins, and looped them over the top of the hames. Clarence had followed the same procedure with the mare. Grabbing the sides of the bridles, father and son backed the two horses out of their stalls. As they led the horses from the stable, Old Gray, a third horse, whinnied as if begging not to be left out. Hinman reminded her that she'd get her chance when it was time to begin raking. Once outside, the horses side by side, Hinman threaded Sally's short inside rein through the ring in the spreader and snapped it to the gelding's outside rein and vice versa.

Before he hitched the team to the mowing machine, Hinman made sure that the drive mechanism was disengaged. If it were still engaged and the team were to lurch forward, the wooden shaft called the pitman might break. Hinman drove the team alongside the pole of the mower and coaxed Sally to step over the pole into place. Hinman hooked the free ends of the traces to the whiffletree. Leading each horse forward a step or two, Hinman and Clarence snapped the rings from the neck yokes to the yoke straps hanging from the collar. Once the team was hitched to the mower, Hinman climbed into the cast-iron seat and carefully arranged the reins in his hands. He made a clucking sound, snapped the reins, and started the team forward.

On the way to the hayfield Hinman kept the cutter bar in a vertical position so that it could pass easily through the

Farmer's right hand presses down on lever to raise cutter bar.

gate. Once inside, he stopped the team and, removing the wing nut from the brace, lowered the cutter bar to the horizontal position several inches above the ground.

Resuming his seat on the mower, Hinman engaged its gears with the foot pedal on the left side and lowered the cutter bar still further by using the lever on the right. A "giddap" started the team around the field in a clockwise direction. The rotation of the mower wheels transferred power through the gears to the flywheel. The pitman was attached to the flywheel on an off-centered axis so that the flywheel's rotary motion was converted into the reciprocating motion of the pitman. This caused the section to move back and forth. The section knives cut the grass against the stationary blades of the guards on the cutter bar.

The team proceeded at a brisk walk, and a five-foot-wide swath of grass fell behind the cutter bar. In their first circuit of the field, the horses walked through uncut grass; after that they traveled on the hay cut the previous time around.

As he drove the team, Hinman monitored the condition of the hay and the workings of the mower. If the grass was coarse and upright, the mower sharp, and the field free from obstructions, he enjoyed the pleasures that monotony affords; the acrobatics of field mice scrambling for cover, the clownish strut of crows in search of gourmet delights exposed in the new-mown hay, or the lulling "ra-ta-ta-ta" of the cutter bar. Occasionally he added oil to the oil cups.

Hinman, however, could not afford to daydream. When he approached an obstruction—a low rock, stump, or woodchuck mound—he raised the cutter bar just before reaching it and then lowered the cutter bar as soon as the obstacle was passed. He had to watch for woodchuck holes that could cripple the horse that stepped into one. He drove around higher obstacles, such as big rocks, stumps, and trees. To ignore them might mean broken section knives, bent guards, a broken pitman, or a cracked tongue.

Another potential problem was a clogged cutter bar, which caused the mower wheels to lock and skid. If this happened, Hinman quickly halted the team and pulled the lever back, raising the cutter bar above the mown hay. A sharp command and the team backed the mower several feet, with the ratchet clicking in the drive mechanism. Then Hinman started the horses forward in hopes that the cutter bar would free up. If it did, Hinman lowered the cutter bar just as it entered unmown grass and continued mowing. If not, he dismounted and removed the clogging grass by hand.

If the team edged too close to the unmown grass, the inner shoe of the mower bent that grass down, leaving uncut strips, called manes. These strips were clearly visible after the hay was raked from the field, a sign of sloppy mowing and an embarrassment to the serious mower.

When starting a field it was possible to mow the wide corners, but as they got tighter Hinman had to stop at the end of each swath, raise the cutter bar, and then sidestep the horses the quarter turn. Then he lowered the cutter bar and went on. While he was mowing, Albert and Clarence, pitchforks in hand, shook out any bunched hay they found at the corners of the fields where the cutter bar had swung back or where their father had backed up to unclog it.[6]

After two hours Hinman finished mowing the field except for an uncut strip around the outside, now sprung back from where the horses and mower had bent it. Raising the cutter bar and kicking the drive mechanism out of gear, he drove to the outside of the field. Lowering the cutter bar and engaging the mower, he sent the team in a counterclockwise direction, cutting the swath that had been left in his initial pass.

At the gate, he disengaged the mower and put the cutter bar in the vertical position, securing it with the rod and wing nut. He then left the team in a shady spot while he and the boys trimmed the edges and corners of the field with scythes. When they finished, it was almost noon, so Charles drove to the barn, where he unhitched the team and led the sweat-soaked horses to their stalls. He allowed them only a little not-too-cold water; too much could cause colic. He removed their bridles but left on the harness. After putting on their halters, he gave each horse some grain and hay.[7]

The Hinmans washed up and sat down to the main meal of the day—sausages, new potatoes and peas, bread and butter, and rhubarb pie. After dinner Charles and the boys rested in the shade on the front lawn for half an hour.[8]

About a quarter to one Hinman signaled the boys that it was work time. That afternoon they mowed about two more acres of another field; they did not want to get more hay down than they could make the next day. Hinman left the mower in the field and drove the team back to the barn.

The next morning, after chores and breakfast, Hinman finished the field he had started the day before. At ten o'clock he checked the hay he had cut the previous morning. The hot July sun had dried the hay on top of the swath but the grass at the bottom still felt moist and flexible.

Hinman asked Albert to hitch up Old Gray to the tedder. Once in the field, Albert drove Old Gray around it in the same direction in which his father had mowed. The six small forks at the rear of the tedder kicked up the hay, turning and fluffing it to facilitate drying. He had to be obser-

The hay tedder absorbs the shock of hitting large stones.

vant, for while the spring teeth of the tedder were able to absorb the shock of hitting small rocks or hummocks, a large obstruction could cause damage. Although Old Gray was approaching the end of her usefulness, tedding was one task she could still do. A tedder is light and easy for a horse to pull. Albert had the field tedded before dinner.

By early afternoon the hay that had been cut the morning before was dry enough to rake. A horse-drawn dump rake can do the work of eight or ten men raking by hand. A single horse and driver can rake twenty to thirty acres of hay in a day without too much effort. Hinman's ten-year-old daughter Nellie was assigned this task. Albert hitched Old Gray to the dump rake and, holding the rake teeth in the up position, drove down to the field. There he dismounted and helped Nellie onto the seat. Nellie called "Giddap," and Old Gray started down the outside of the field in a clockwise direction. When Nellie figured the rake was full enough, she stepped on the small foot pedal that engaged the dumping mechanism. As soon as the rake was clear of the pile of hay, the teeth dropped to the ground.[9]

Occasionally the rake got too full and pulled some of the hay after it. These "draggy tails" were a reminder to Nellie to dump sooner. On the second and subsequent circuits of the field Nellie lined up each pile with an earlier one to form a windrow, perpendicular to the edge of the field. After Nellie had raked at least four times around the field, Clarence began to tumble the windrows.

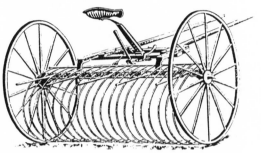

Spring-toothed dump rake.

In the barn Hinman and Albert hitched Sally and the gelding to the hay wagon. Mr. Carpenter volunteered to make the load for them, and the three rode on the hayrack to the hayfield. There Mr. Carpenter guided the team down the "road" between the rows of tumbles and brought the horses to a halt when the first tumbles were abreast of the front of the hay wagon. Hinman and Albert picked up their pitchforks from the wagon bed as Mr. Carpenter tied the reins to the pole at the front of the hayrack.

The loading began at the rear of the wagon as each pitcher placed one tumble in the space between the spindles. Mr. Carpenter might make minor adjustments in these placements with his own fork. Once the rack was filled level with the sideboards, the men built the top part of the load three tumbles wide.

Moving to the front of the wagon, each pitcher placed a tumble in each of its two front corners. Then each placed another tumble directly behind the first, overlapping it slightly. Taking Hinman's third tumble, Mr. Carpenter positioned it in the front center so that it overlapped the first two corner tumbles. He then placed Albert's third tumble between the second pair of side tumbles. The three men continued their smooth teamwork, steadily placing tumbles on either side of the load and binding them with center tumbles. When room remained on this layer, or round, for only two more tumbles on either side, Mr. Carpenter placed the next to the last side tumble in the rear corner. The last side tumble, known as a binder, held this corner in

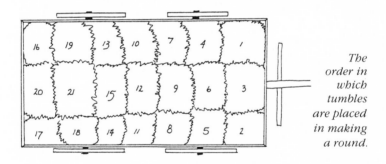

The order in which tumbles are placed in making a round.

place. A binder in the rear center held the two corner tumbles. He then set a final center tumble, which held the two side binders in place. The first round finished, he began the second round at the rear and worked his way forward.[10]

While loading, Mr. Carpenter drove the wagon slowly along the "road" to keep up with the two pitchers who were advancing from one windrow to another. Since Sally was trained to respond to voice command, he did not have to move constantly to the front of the wagon to drive the team with the reins. From time to time Mr. Carpenter yelled "gee" or "haw" to keep the horses in the center of the road, just as Dr. Shattuck had fifty years earlier. Frequently one horse would try to nibble at a tumble and pull the wagon sideways. Moreover, the gelding was quicker than Sally and did more than his share of the work. Consequently he worked the load toward Sally's side. Mr. Carpenter constantly corrected these wanderings.[11]

On the ground Hinman and Albert pitched at a steady, unhurried pace. They used their torsos to do much of the work. By anchoring the hand that held the end of the fork handle against his hip and using this point as a fulcrum, the pitcher could raise the forkful of hay into the air by merely arching his back.

If a youngster were pitching, the man making the load, who had the easier job, helped by reaching out and inserting his fork into the raised tumble, lifting it off the pitcher's fork, and placing it on the load. (A strong pitcher could, of course, pitch directly onto the load.) When assisting the pitcher, it was considered bad form for the loader to snare the pitcher's fork with his own so as to yank it out of his hands.[12]

The pitching and loading continued until five or six rounds were completed. The load was topped off with an extra row of tumbles down the center. The number of rounds depended on the type of grass involved and the distance to be traveled. If there was much witch grass, which is slippery, a small load was advisable. Clover, on the other hand, sticks together well and allows large loads.[13]

From his perch on top, the driver taking the completed load to the barn had to watch that tree branches did not sweep him off. Approaching the barn, Mr. Carpenter centered the wagon on the covered ramp, so that it would not get hung up. He ducked as the load went through the doorway, urged the team up the grade, and stopped them quickly once they reached the high drive inside. Hinman and Albert slid off the load and climbed into the mow.

Ideally a load was pitched off by the same person who loaded it because he knew where he had put each tumble. It was unloaded in exactly the reverse order, tumble by tumble, into the mow or hayloft. Mr. Carpenter, on top of the load, started with the last tumble he had placed. To pick any other would mean that he would have to pull it out from under another tumble. He then moved down the center as if he were unzipping the load. He tossed each tumble into the mow where Hinman either placed it with his pitchfork or transferred it to Albert, who stood further back. They filled the mow level and packed it firmly.

The load emptied, Hinman and Albert climbed out of the mow, soaked with sweat, and mopped their brows. Mr. Carpenter, reins in hand, backed the team. As long as the horses backed up straight the wagon did the same, and once on the ramp its weight helped keep it straight. But this time Sally moved too slowly and the wagon's tail veered to the left. Mr. Carpenter drove the team forward until the wagon was again aligned and then guided it to firm ground.[14] He stopped at the house to pick up a jug of switchel and headed to the field for another load.

Loading hay on a sidehill, as he was doing now, demanded special skill. It was important to drive the wagon along the side of the hill rather than up and down. To pull a partial or full load uphill was too strenuous for the horses. Since farm wagons had no brakes, it was also difficult, if not dangerous, to handle a loaded wagon headed downhill. To load with the hayrack on a sideways slant, however, could make the load lopsided—higher on the downhill side. Fortunately, Mr. Carpenter's experience allowed him to compensate for the slant.

29.

Hinman pitched from the downhill side, since that was a longer and harder pitch than from the uphill side. The load was limited to fewer rounds because of the danger of its sliding off. When the load was finished and the team had been driven to level ground, it was obvious why very few of Mr. Carpenter's loads ever fell off—they were pretty level.

That afternoon they got in four loads. Before heading for their last one, Hinman had asked Nellie to get the cows and drive them to the barn. By the time the last forkful was mowed away, it was choretime. As Hinman entered the stable he was pleased to find the cows in their stanchions. Clarence had begun milking.

After chores came supper, which was almost as substantial as the noon meal. Before darkness fell they brought three more loads to the barn. While the boys helped, Nellie raked the scatterings.

Throughout July and early August they hayed whenever the weather permitted. Despite the spring predictions of crop failure, the hay crop was the biggest and best Mr. Carpenter could remember. He wrote to his grandchildren, "Our barns were never so full before. I think certainly three or four tons more than last year." He estimated they had harvested forty-six tons from their twenty-three acres of hayland.[15]

With the help of horse-powered machinery in every operation except the loading and unloading of the hay, two men and three children were able to put up fifty percent more hay than Marshall Castle had put up half a century earlier. The only change in the loading was that a horse-drawn wagon could carry more than an oxcart and horses moved at a livelier pace.

Hayloader and Horse Fork

Wellman Rowell 1934

The best hay crop in several years is being harvested by the farmers of Orleans County. In spite of the great labor shortage the farmers are getting on well with haying as many have purchased labor saving machinery such as side-delivery rakes, hay loaders and horse forks.

August 8, 1923[1]
Orleans County Monitor

Marshall Carpenter died in the spring of 1883 and his brother Chester, Jr., bought the farm from the estate. Eleven years later Chester sold it to his son-in-law, Myron Adams, one of Vermont's leading dairymen. As the years passed, the farm changed hands several more times.[2]

Along with changes in ownership, there were also changes in the buildings and in prevalent dairying and haying methods. Dairying was shifting from the production of cheese and butter to the shipment of fluid milk in refrigerated railcars. Herds were larger and needed more hay. But there was no increase in the availability of labor. In fact, farm labor was scarce. Farmers were faced with the need to get in more hay in the same amount of time with less help.

In 1934 while the nation was in the grip of the Great Depression, the old Carpenter farm was in the hands of Mr. and Mrs. Wellman Rowell. They ran it with the help of their fourteen-year-old son Kenneth, nicknamed Billy, and two hired men. One, Buster Bowen, lived with his wife in the older part of the farmhouse; the other, Roy Fournier, boarded with the Rowell family. Mrs. Rowell worked full-time as a bookkeeper at the Clyde Valley Creamery, which was one mile away at the head of the road, while Grandmother Rowell, who also lived on the farm, cared for four-year-old Barbara and helped with the housework. During haying, Wellman hired an extra man, Rob.[3]

The Rowells had purchased the farm in 1928 and had initially followed haying methods similar to those used by Charles Hinman fifty years earlier. Soon, however, Wellman Rowell began to make big changes. He installed electricity in the farmhouse and barn; this allowed him to acquire milking machines, running water in his stables, and a refrigeration unit for his milk cooler. He purchased a McCormick-Deering tractor. By the early thirties he had adopted the system of hay handling that included the side-delivery rake, hayloader, and horse fork. In 1934 he bought a one-and-a-half ton Chevrolet truck with a long wheel base.[4]

Acquisition of a tractor did not eliminate horses from the farm. Wellman customarily kept at least two and frequently four. At that time almost all farm implements were designed to be horse-drawn. The tractor was faster, did not tire, had more power, and could drive stationary machinery that required pulley power, but these advantages could not be realized unless the machinery was adapted for tractor use. Certain implements wore out or flew apart because of the tractor's higher speed. Wellman did not use his tractor to mow. It required two men; one to drive and the other to operate the mowing machine, whereas one man could drive a team of horses and at the same time operate the mower from its seat.

Hayloader picks up hay from continuous windrow.

In the summer of 1934 haying began for Wellman Rowell much as it had fifty years earlier for Charles Hinman. In preparation he did the regular greasing and maintenance checks on the implements; this included sharpening the mower sections. One new task was to build extensions on both sides of the truck body to permit larger loads.

While the new haying system that Wellman had recently adopted was designed for horse power, it was readily adaptable to motor power with no loss in effectiveness. This allowed him the flexibility of using both. The new system required more horse power, and farmers were buying larger horses. While the old dump rake usually needed only one horse, the new side-delivery rake always required a team of two horses, as did the hayloader.

In early July Wellman began his mowing with a horse-drawn machine that had changed little since Charles Hinman's time. Wellman was able, however, to down more hay that first day, because he had the capacity to pick it up faster the next. Rob and Billy tedded the corners with pitch-forks; Buster and Roy trimmed the edge of the field with scythes.

After the evening chores Wellman's son hitched the tractor to the side-delivery rake. The new practice was to rake the new-mown hay just before night, so that less of it was exposed to the dew.[5] The side-delivery rake acceler-ated drying and caused less damage to the leaves. It lifted the grass from the swath and deposited it in loose, fluffy windrows with the leaves inside. The air circulated easily through them.

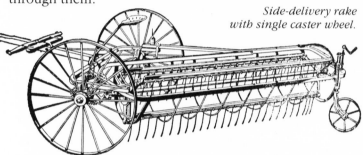

Side-delivery rake with single caster wheel.

The side-delivery rake was different from the dump rake. On the dump rake a row of teeth perpendicular to the direction of travel dragged along the ground until it was full of hay, at which time it was raised to dump the hay in a pile and then lowered again. The side-delivery rake, on the other hand, consisted of a rotating reel set about forty-five degrees from the direction of travel. The reel was composed of four horizontal rake bars with rows of teeth attached. The rake had two large drive wheels, which pro-vided power to rotate the reel, and two small caster wheels that supported the rear.

Before Billy climbed into the driver's seat, he made sure that the drive wheels were disengaged from the reel and that the tooth-adjusting lever was in the back notch, which raised the teeth above the strippers out of reach of damaging obstacles.[6] Once in the field, Billy engaged the drive mechanism, moved the tooth-adjusting lever forward to the fourth notch, and made sure that the front-lifting lever was in the center notch. The teeth were set as high as possible and yet still able to lift the hay gently and leave the windrows loose so the air could move through them.

Billy started raking down the outside of the hayfield. The tractor, centered on the swath being raked, traveled in a clockwise direction. Glancing back, Billy noticed that the teeth were hitting the ground. He stopped the tractor, dismounted, and raised the teeth slightly by moving the lever back to the fifth notch. This prevented the teeth from kicking dirt into the windrow and lessened the wear on the rake.

Once adjusted, the side-delivery rake was easy to operate. Billy drove the tractor around the field, making one continuous windrow that spiraled in toward the center. The bottom of the reel swept forward, lifting the hay and moving it to the left into a windrow. He did not have to judge when the rake was full nor activate the dumping mechanism when he lined up with the previous windrow. Nor did he have to take pains with the corners of the field. With the side-delivery rake it was just a matter of steering the tractor.

The side-delivery rake was essential for use with a hayloader. The windrows left by a dump rake were usually perpendicular to the line of travel of the hay wagon. On the other hand, the hayloader required a windrow parallel to the direction of travel. Secondly, the side-delivery rake twisted the hay into a roll like a loose strand of rope. This twist facilitated the hay's travel up the loader.[7] Within an hour the field was raked. Since he would use the rake again the next morning, Billy left it and the tractor in the field and walked home.

The next morning when the dew was almost off the grass, Billy and Buster went back to the field. They had to adjust the rake so that instead of raking up loose hay, it would turn over an existing windrow. They slid the left front wheel of the rake in on the axle. Now the reel extended a foot or so beyond the wheel. As the wheel ran next to the right-hand edge of the windrow the rake inverted the windrow, placing it on dry stubble and exposing the damp hay from the bottom to the sun and breeze. While Billy turned the windrows in yesterday's piece, Wellman mowed another field. If the day were hot and dry, the hay that he had mown the day before would be ready to load by mid-afternoon. If it had rained, however, it was often necessary to turn the windrows several times before they were thoroughly cured and ready for loading.

Toward afternoon Wellman checked the condition of the hay that Billy had turned that morning and was satisfied that it was sufficiently cured. Since there was a lot of hay down and he did not want to risk leaving it overnight, he decided to use both the truck and the horse-drawn hay wagon for picking it up.[8] After dinner he and Billy hitched the hayloader behind the truck, while Buster and Roy harnessed the team and hitched them to the hay wagon. Billy

Hayloader with slatted conveyor.

positioned the tractor beside the barn ramp and attached it to the rope from the horse fork that they would use to unload the hay.

Once in the field Billy and his father got out and lowered the hayloader's gathering cylinder by turning the hand nuts on the adjusting rod on both sides. The gathering cylinder works best in the highest position in which it will rake cleanly. If set too high, it misses some hay; if too low, it scrapes the ground, throwing dust into the hay.[9]

After engaging the drive wheels of the hayloader, Rowell climbed onto the truck body and grabbed his hayfork, while Billy took his seat in the cab. He steered so that the truck straddled the windrow. As the main wheels of the hayloader turned, their sprockets drove chains that powered the gathering cylinder, the elevating cylinder, and the conveyor belt. The gathering cylinder, rotating so that the teeth swept the hay forward, combed the stubble to pick up the hay and passed it on to the elevating cylinder, which transferred it to the rope-and-slat conveyor belt. The belt raised the hay to the top of the hayloader where it then dropped onto the truck body.

The pace of loading was slightly faster than when the hay was hand-pitched, but the hay did not come on in neat tumbles. Hence, making a load was not quite as methodical as before. On the other hand, the load did not have to be made so precisely, because the horse fork unloaded in large bundles instead of tumble by tumble. Nonetheless, Wellman still tried to keep the load level and evenly packed so that it would not fall off.

Roy and Buster had driven into the hayfield with the team and wagon and now came up behind the full truck. Wellman pulled the trip rope, which opened the hitch point and disconnected the hayloader from the truck, leaving the loader astraddle the windrow while the truck proceeded toward the barn. Now the horse-drawn hay wagon approached the hayloader from behind. As they passed it, Buster jumped off. Roy cut in sharply and centered the wagon on the windrow in front of the hayloader, backing the team toward it while Buster held up the hitch. The click of the hitch indicated that the hayloader was attached to the wagon. Buster climbed aboard; Roy snapped the reins and yelled "Giddap!" Another load began streaming onto the hayrack.

The team had to strain at first; the two horses were not only pulling the wagon and hayloader, they were also providing power through the traction wheels to run the gathering cylinder, elevating cylinder, and conveyor of the loader. When the wagon was full, they would be pulling up to a ton of hay.

Meanwhile, Billy drove the truck up the barn ramp and stopped with the load directly under the horse fork. He climbed down and started the tractor attached to the rope of the horse fork. The extra hired hand jumped into the lower mow where he spent the afternoon mowing away the hay as it was unloaded.

A horse fork is a device that works with either harpoons or grapples to remove large bundles of hay from a wagon or truck. It is suspended from a carrier high in the ridge of the roof. The two-pronged fork can move the length of the barn on a track hanging from the ridge. Wellman had jabbed the double-harpoon

Double-harpoon horse fork.

Grapple horse fork.

fork into the centerline of the load, toward the back. Once the horse fork is inserted into the load, two toggles at its tips turn at right angles, securing the hay. When Wellman called "Okay,"

Billy drove

the tractor away from the barn.

The rope pulled about one-quarter of the load straight up to the carrier. When the fork reached the top, it locked into the carrier. Further tension on the rope pulled the carrier toward the end of the barn. When the load was where he wanted it, Wellman pulled the trip line and yelled "Whoa!" to stop Billy from pulling the rope further. The toggles of the fork straightened and released the hay, which

Horse fork carrier.

fell into the mow. The man in the mow used a pitchfork to distribute it to the sides and corners, so that the barn filled evenly.[10]

Pulling the trip line, Wellman returned the carrier to the center of the barn and Billy backed the tractor to

The track on which the carrier rides hangs from the underside of the barn ridge.

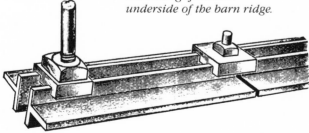

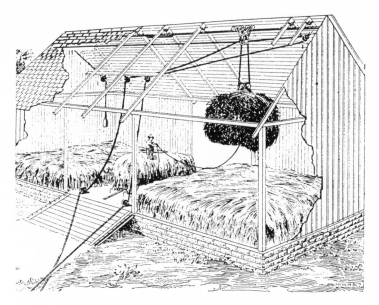

With a trip line the farmer releases hay onto the mow.

give slack to the rope. When the carrier was centered, the fork was released from the carrier and began to descend. Wellman grabbed it; when there was enough slack, he repeated the unloading process.

Two forkfuls later the truck was empty except for some loose ends that Wellman quickly pitched into the mow. Billy backed the truck out of the barn as Roy and Buster approached with another load. That afternoon the two crews got in fourteen loads before it was time to do chores. While Wellman and the two hired men milked, Billy raked the piece that had been mowed that morning.

After three days the east mow was full to ten feet above the level of the high drive. Billy climbed a ladder and swiveled the fork carrier so that it could travel to the west mow. When both mows in the big barn were full, they moved to the mow over the south stable. The horse fork in this barn loaded through a bottom-hinged door at the end of the barn. The door hung down against the barn's side, and the track for the horse fork extended outside the barn's end. They parked the truck or wagon under the horse fork.

By the end of July the first cutting was finished. The men had put in close to one hundred tons of hay. In late August they took the rowen, or second cutting, from the better fields, but allowed the cattle to graze the others.

The introduction of the hayloader and the horse fork completed the mechanization of haying; every operation was assisted by either horse power or the tractor. With a crew the same size as that used by Marshall Castle a hundred years earlier, Wellman Rowell had been able to put in three times as much hay. And he had harvested twice as much as Charles Hinman had fifty years before.

Haybine and Baler

Donald Kilborn, Jr., 1982

B y the 1980s the farm on which Marshall Carpenter and Wellman Rowell and others had supported their families was out of business, like so many family farms in America. After a period of abandonment, the place was purchased by people from "away." They loved country living, but did not make their living from the land.

The pastures were growing into forest, and the hayland had been planted to pine and fir. The new family repaired the house and reclaimed some of the fields, but the barns were empty and in disrepair.

Farming was still, however, important to the economy of the community. Just up the road Don Kilborn, Jr., was actively engaged in dairying. Kilborn, a bachelor in his fifties, ran the family farm he had acquired from his father. With Wilfred Tetreault, a young man who worked for him full-time, year-round, Kilborn milked forty cows. Although his was a modest-size operation by 1982 standards, Kilborn kept up with the latest in dairying technology.

At the Kilborn farm in early April the snow was still on the ground. As the drifts slowly melted and more of the ground opened to the warming rays of the sun, Don and Willy readied themselves for a busy six-month season of growing and gathering. The snow was followed by mud season, when the fields were too soft to work. Mud season is traditionally a time to repair fences before the cows are let out. As soon as the ground is firm manure is spread on the cornfields, which must then be plowed, harrowed, and planted by the end of May.

When spring arrives in Vermont nature bursts upon the scene as if it knew it had but a few short months before another winter. To Don it seemed that it took the trees no more than a week to go from bare branches to full foliage. Brown fields were soon luxuriant with clover, timothy, and alfalfa. By the first week of June the grass had almost headed out. Don would begin mowing in the next few days.

The process of harvesting grass had changed dramatically since Wellman Rowell's time a half-century earlier. Although Don still put up some hay, he fed most of his forage in the form of silage, chopped grass that has a higher moisture content than hay, is easier to harvest, more palatable, and retains more nutrients.

As silage, grass went from the field to the cow's stomach through a totally mechanized system. The grass was cut, picked up, and blown mechanically into the blue Harvestore silo. When it was time to feed silage to the cows, Don merely flicked the switch, and the electrical silo-unloader delivered it to the feed troughs from which the cows ate.[1]

The amount of equipment on the Kilborn farm was impressive. There were five tractors: an International 656 (an 85-horsepower diesel), a four-wheel drive Italian-built Same 85, a Ford diesel tractor with bucket, a 1944 gas-powered International H, and a small Ford 1600 diesel for scraping the manure out of the stables. For the harvesting of grass silage Kilborn used a New Holland 474 haybine with a seven-foot cutter bar, a New Holland forage harvester with grass pick-up head, two Kasten self-unloading forage wagons, and an International silage blower at the base of the silo. In addition to the haybine, Don's haying equipment included a Kuhn tedder, an International rake, a New Holland 311 baler with kicker, and two hay wagons with racks. In 1982 the replacement value of this equipment would have been about $122,400, a considerable investment. He stored his machinery in a large enclosed shed. Always conscientious about maintenance, each fall he put away each implement in perfect repair, so there was little to do in preparation for harvesting. His New Holland haybine was only a year old, and his baler was brand-new.[2]

Because the grass was late in maturing this year, Don did not start mowing until June 11. Usually he would have begun a week earlier. Fortunately, he had scheduled his grass silage harvest before his haymaking. Much of the hay put up by other farmers that June would be of poor quality because of the frequent rains. Wet weather had less effect on silage since that grass was harvested at a higher moisture content and therefore did not have to dry so long, exposed to the threat of rain.

On the morning of June 11, Don Kilborn was up by 5:00 A.M. as usual. Although the sun was not up, the sky was light and Don was pleased that it was cloudless. In the barnyard stood three or four cows, which he drove into the freestall area of the barn where the other cows waited. Cows accounted for, he set up the three milking machines

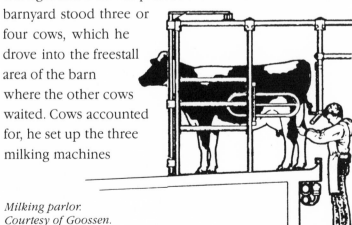

Milking parlor.
Courtesy of Goossen.

in the four-stall milking parlor. Opening the door at the rear of the parlor, he admitted three cows. Each cow was grained, her udder was washed and massaged to stimulate the release of milk, and a milking machine was attached. Almost immediately milk spurted into the glass weigh jars, which were calibrated to show how much milk each cow gave. As each cow was milked out, Don removed the machine, opened the door, and let the cow walk away. At about six o'clock Willy showed up to feed the calves and help Don. Within an hour the milking was finished. Willy and Don cleaned the parlor and milking equipment; then they drove the cows to pasture across the road. With his Ford 1600 tractor Don scraped the freestall alleys clean of manure and pushed it into a pit at the end of the barn. From there a piston pumped it into a Slurrystore manure tank where it was stored until Don was ready to spread it on the fields. By 7 A.M. the chores were finished and the two men headed home for breakfast: Willy to his parents' house two doors down and Don to his own breakfast of cold cereal with milk and maple syrup, toast, and coffee.[3]

Outdoors again, Don turned the ignition key on his Same 85 tractor. Almost immediately there was a puff of smoke and the engine roared to life. He stepped on the clutch, shifted into gear, and drove to the fuel pump where he topped off the tank with diesel fuel. At the equipment shed, he shifted into reverse and backed the tractor toward the tongue of the haybine. The tractor's power steering enabled him to make an easy line-up of the tractor drawbar and the haybine tongue. A jack on the haybine's tongue held the hitch at the proper height so the drawbar slid into it. When Don estimated that the hole in the drawbar was lined up with the holes in the tongue, he put the tractor in neutral, set the brake, and dismounted. After a little wiggling of the drawbar and hitch, he dropped the pin in place. As he cranked the handle of the jack, its base lifted off the ground. Don swung the jack up alongside the tongue and locked it out of the way.

Reaching for the haybine's power take-off (PTO) shaft, Don telescoped it toward the tractor. He rotated it slowly so that the splines lined up, held the spline lockbutton down, and pushed the haybine's PTO shaft forward until the click told him it was locked onto the tractor's PTO shaft. He then plugged the haybine's hydraulic line into the tractor's hydraulic system and remounted the tractor.

Raising the cutterhead hydraulically, he carefully eased the haybine out of the shed. As he drove to the field, he kept the haybine in the transport position with its tongue locked to the right so that the implement trailed behind the tractor. Since the haybine was almost ten feet wide, Don used his emergency flashers when driving on the road; the haybine's right wheel hugged the shoulder.

The face of the land had changed considerably since Marshall Castle's time. Subsequent farmers had blasted or bulldozed boulders, picked smaller stones, and removed fencerows to make larger fields with fewer obstructions. In recent years Don had ditched or tiled several wet spots so that his heavier equipment would not get stuck and to allow the crops to grow better.[4]

In the field to be mowed, Don brought the tractor to a halt. Reaching back, he grabbed the lanyard attached to the haybine's tongue-latch, pulled it, and backed the tractor to the left. This swung the tongue until it locked in the left position. In this position the haybine's cutterhead was completely to the right of the tractor's right tire, free to mow grass that had not been bent by the tractor's wheels. To avoid the necessity of raking, he had set the deflectors of the haybine to form a narrow windrow. While the extra thickness would increase the time necessary to dry the grass to the desired fifty percent moisture content, continued dry weather would eliminate raking. If Don wanted to hurry the drying process, he could adjust the haybine to deposit the hay in a broader swath, ted the swath after a few hours, and rake it into windrows just before picking it up.

Don engaged the PTO. After glancing back to check that everything was working properly, he lowered the cutterhead and started forward, cutting a seven-foot swath of grass at a speed of four to five miles per hour.[5] A bar pushed the grass forward so that when it was cut the butts of the stalks were fed into the crushing rolls. The coil-spring fingers of the pickup reel are especially important if the grass has been blown down or tangled; they comb the grass over the cutter bar and into two fluted rubber rolls, which crimp and crack the stems at intervals so that the moisture in the grass can escape.

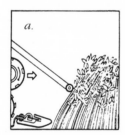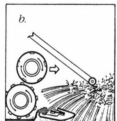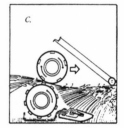

a. Haybine bar pushes grass forward. b. Mower guard (at ground level) severs grass stalks. c. Grass crushed by rubber rolls. Courtesy of International.

The first time around the field in a clockwise direction, Don tried to get the left tire of the tractor as close to the field's edge as possible without hitting the brush, fences, or ditches that formed its boundaries. In the second and subsequent passes he guided the tractor so that the left end of the cutter bar was at the border between mown and unmown grass.

Don drove with his head turned slightly to the right. By glancing ahead he could see how far it was to the next turn and whether he was headed in the right direction. Looking backward he could ensure that the haybine was aligned with the edge of the grass. A slight movement of the power steering corrected any deviation from the mark. Out of the corner of his right eye Don caught the blur of the rotating PTO shaft, and he heard the slight rattle of its safety shields. In his mid-vision was the slow rotation of the reel swishing the grass over the clattering cutter bar. His left ear took in the subdued roar of the 85-horsepower diesel engine.

The sun's rays warmed the tops of his thighs and back of his neck and shoulders—rays that had already turned his neck and arms a deep reddish-brown. Don was thankful for the cooling breeze that stirred the maples beside the field.

The power steering swung the tractor so that the haybine pivoted easily at each wide corner. As the corners grew tighter, however, Don raised the cutterhead at the end of each pass and then swung the tractor in a 270° arc. This enabled him to mow at right angles to the previous pass. He lowered the cutter-head just as the haybine entered unmown hay. If the field was narrower than it was

Mowing with a haybine. Courtesy of Ford-New Holland.

50.

long, a point came where it was not worth the effort to mow the short leg. Then Don raised the cutterhead just as it finished one swath and swung a wide 180° arc to the right to cross to the other side of the mowing. He mowed as much grass as he figured he could pick up the next afternoon.

The next morning Don mowed more grass. That afternoon he drove the Same to the field he had mowed the morning before, pulling the forage harvester and forage wagon behind him. Willy attached the International 656 to the stationary silage blower, then left the barnyard with the Ford and a second forage wagon.

Don lowered the pickup head of the forage harvester and drove clockwise around the field. The head picked up the grass in the windrows and fed it into the chopper, which blew the chopped grass through the pipe into the trailing forage wagon. When the first wagon was full, Willy and Don switched wagons. Willy pulled the full wagon toward the silo while Don resumed chopping. The Harvestore silo would hold approximately two-thirds of the grass harvested on the farm. In addition, Kilborn had a concrete silo for storing his corn silage.

At the silo Willy maneuvered the wagon so that its discharge chute was over the hopper of the silage blower. He jumped from the Ford, started the 656, and engaged the PTO that drove the blower. Returning to the Ford, he engaged its PTO, and the forage harvester began to discharge chopped grass into the hopper of the silage blower. From there the grass was blown up the filler tube into the top of the silo. Discharged, the grass fell into the silo. The forage wagon emptied, Willy turned off the tractor that powered the blower and returned to the field to get another load.

The silage harvesting continued for the next three weeks; they cut grass in the mornings and filled the silo in the afternoons. By Sunday, July 4, Don dared not put any more into the silo for fear of plugging the blower tube. They would have to bale the remaining grass. The weather prediction out of Montreal promised favorable conditions for drying so Don decided to start haying the next day.

The process of cutting hay was almost identical to harvesting grass silage. The one exception was that the windrow deflector of the haybine was opened so that it deposited the cut grass in a swath the full width of the cutter bar. Since hay must be much drier than silage, it is important that more of the grass be exposed to the sun and breeze, thereby speeding the drying process. Don mowed until he had enough grass down to make between one thousand and twelve hundred bales.

After lunch Willy hitched the International 656 to the Kuhn tedder and went to ted the hay cut that morning. When he moved the tedder between fields, he folded the two outer rotors forward so that the machine was narrow enough to fit through gates. Once in the field Willy swung out the rotors. Mounting the tractor, he engaged the PTO and shifted into third gear, high range. The tedder rotors began to twirl as the tractor moved forward at a speed of four to six miles per hour. Counting from the driver's left, rotors one and three moved in a clockwise direction and

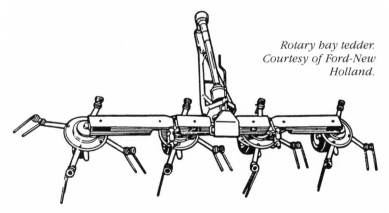

*Rotary hay tedder.
Courtesy of Ford-New
Holland.*

rotors two and four moved counterclockwise. The rotor tines picked up every blade of grass in an eight-foot path and bent the stems as the grass passed between the two pairs of opposite-turning rotors and fell in a wide, fluffy swath for the sun and wind to dry. Willy started clockwise around the field. Since he was traveling faster than Don had when he mowed, he was able to finish the field in much less time than it had taken Don to cut it. Willy could ted up to four acres an hour.[6]

During chores the next morning Don asked Willy to ted the hay piece again right after breakfast and rake it before lunch, while he mowed another five acres of grass. After tedding, Willy hitched the tractor to the side-delivery rake. The rake swept an eight-foot-wide swath of hay into a windrow to the left. One could rake at the same rate at which one could ted.

Modern traction-powered side-delivery rake. Courtesy of Ford-New Holland.

Finished mowing, Don parked the haybine in the field, unhitched it, and returned to the farmyard for the new baler. It was still in the transport position in which the dealer had left it. By the time Don had finished hitching the baler to his tractor, Willy was driving into the yard for lunch.

After lunch Willy helped Don hitch one hay wagon to the baler. Don drove to the field while Willy hitched the other hay wagon to the International H tractor. Like the haybine, the baler was too wide to travel on the road in its operating position. Therefore, once in the field Don had to adjust the tongue just as he had done with the haybine. This accomplished, he engaged the PTO, lowered the baler pickup, and guided the tractor so that the pickup mechanism was centered on the windrow. The teeth of the pickup mechanism lifted the windrow and moved it up and back into the feed housing. The feeding forks then moved the hay toward the chamber. With the plunger in the return position the forks pushed the charge of hay into the chamber. As the plunger moved in the compression stroke, its knife sheared the hay against a stationary knife, severing the hay in the chamber from the hay still in the feed housing. The plunger continued its stroke, compressing the hay charge. At the end of the stroke, friction held the charge of hay in its compressed state as the plunger returned for another charge. When a set amount of hay was compressed in the chamber, the bale-measuring wheel tripped a mechanism that thrust two needles up through the compressed hay and fed baling twine into the knotting mechanism. Two automatic knotting devices tied overhand knots in the twine, held and cut the twine, and the needles withdrew. The plunger continued to feed compressed hay and pushed the completed bale down the bale chamber. When it hit a trigger the hydraulic piston of the bale kicker grabbed the forty-pound bale and catapulted it in an arc toward the hay wagon.

With the kicker-baler system, a wagon needed high racks on the sides and back to catch the bales as they landed haphazardly. The bales stayed wherever they fell: no one piled them carefully as in earlier days. When the baler turned a corner Don pushed a hydraulic lever that tilted the kicker; the bale then flew to the left and landed as it should in the wagon, which was still turning. As the wagon filled, Don reached back to adjust a crank that lessened the force of the kicker; the bales then fell toward the front of the trailing wagon.

When the wagon could hold no more Don pulled the rope to the "remote wagon detach" and the wagon unhitched and stopped. By this time Willy had brought an empty wagon with the International H. Both men dismounted and hitched the empty wagon behind the baler. Then Don helped Willy hitch his tractor onto the full load, and Willy drove it back to the barn where he tossed the bales into the deep bays. Don used to stack the bales neatly,

Pickup baler without kicker wagon. Courtesy of Ford-New Holland.

but that required the help of two more men. As there was plenty of room, Don economized by throwing the bales in randomly.

After three days of cutting, tedding, raking, and baling, Don and Willy finished haying. They had put in approximately 4,500 bales or 180 tons. Because Don mainly fed corn and grass silage, he would have surplus hay to sell. In a few weeks the cows were turned out into some of the hayfields. A second cutting would go into the silo as the silage already there settled and freed up space.

Don Kilborn fed less baled hay than his predecessors and used more corn and grass silage. Still, he and Willy put in almost twice as much hay as Wellman Rowell had in much less time and with much less effort, thanks to the tractor-powered haybine and kicker-baler system. Only the unloading of the bales required manual labor; all other operations were done by tractor power.

Round Bales and the Milk Factory

Nelson Farms 1990

Today the distinction between hay and silage is becoming blurred. In the 1980s many Vermont farmers shifted from small rectangular bales of forty to sixty pounds to round bales that weighed up to seven hundred pounds. Bales that heavy are a sign that human muscle no longer plays a role in hay harvesting. The round bales are so big that only hydraulic loaders and special trailers can move them. They are designed for outdoor storage, meant to eliminate the capital investment needed for barn storage. There is some waste as the exteriors weather, but the savings in labor and storage are considered worth the loss. To prevent even this spoilage, systems were developed to encase the round bales in plastic. If the hay in them was baled with a slightly higher than normal moisture content before being wrapped in plastic, the grass fermented and became silage. Soon the countryside was dotted with what appeared to be giant marshmallows.

Don Kilborn never converted to round bales. In 1987 Willy Tetreault announced that he wanted to leave farming for a job in construction. Faced with the loss of his only help, Don decided to sell his cows. But he kept most of his equipment in case Willy changed his mind. In 1990 Don still owned the land, but the barns were empty and the fields rented to a neighboring farmer. Now only one working farm survived on the northern slopes of Kilborn Hill where fifty years ago there were seven, and as recently as ten years ago, there were still five.[1]

While the number of farms in Vermont has decreased dramatically, one cannot accurately say that dairying is on the decline. In 1987 Orleans County still had 408 farms milking 27,589 cows. While this represented only nineteen percent of the number of farms that had existed in the county in 1930, there had been only a four percent decline in the number of cows. The quantity of milk produced actually increased by 250 percent. Through improved feeding and selective breeding the average cow in 1987 produced two-and-a-half times as much milk as it did in 1930. The surviving farms have, on average, twice the acreage, over four times the number of cows, and produce twelve times the amount of milk.[2]

Across the valley from Don Kilborn's farm, in the center of Derby Village, stands one of the farms belonging to Doug Nelson. This farm, which might best be described as a milk factory, may represent the future of dairying in Vermont. Housed under one roof are seven hundred dairy cows. Two shifts of workers operate the milking parlor sixteen to eighteen hours a day. The parlor can handle sixteen cows at a time. Nelson Farms, operated by Nelson and his two sons, milks a total of two thousand cows on three farms in Derby, Derby Line, and Irasburg and employs thirty year-round workers.[3]

Each farm has two men who do the milking, two more who do other barn chores, and a fifth who substitutes for the others on their days off. Five or six men make up the field crew. During planting and harvesting seasons Nelson and his two sons help with the field work. The rest of the time they manage the operation.

A key factor influencing the way Nelson operates is

the shortage of labor. He must try to keep the hours and wages of his workers fairly competitive with those of workers in non-agricultural jobs. His barn workers put in forty to fifty hours per five-and-a-half-day week. During the busy months his field crew works six days, and at peak times some of those days run over fifteen hours long. The men stay on the payroll year round; during the slower winter months, the field crew overhauls equipment.

Nelson Farms operates two trailer tank trucks, which haul all the milk produced on the farms directly to the Cumberland Farms plant in Boston. Every fourteen hours Nelson Farms produces enough milk to fill one of these 8,500-gallon tankers. Their annual output of thirty million pounds of milk represents approximately one and a half percent of Vermont's total milk production.

With a production equal to that of approximately forty average Vermont farms, Nelson Farms benefits from economies of scale. It has, for example, eighteen tractors while forty farms might own at least eighty. This increase in scale, however, requires a massive expenditure of capital. Nelson estimated that his chemical fertilizer alone for 1990 cost approximately $150,000.

The bucket loader on this tractor is used to lift 700-lb. round bales.

This business cultivates two thousand acres of corn and between one thousand and twelve hundred acres of grass for silage, but no longer puts up any hay; it purchases hay from Canada more cheaply than it can produce it. All the cattle have access to some hay; dry cows get more than milkers do, but the herd's primary source of nutrients is silage and grain.

Nelson Farms illustrates how agriculture may be following the same general trends that affected industry during the nineteenth century and have influenced the commercial sector in this century. Increase in the scale of operation, reliance on wage labor, and enhancement of productivity through ever-greater use of technology are all factors that now link the management challenges of modern farms to those of factories and commercial chains.

During the two hundred years of animal husbandry in Vermont, we have seen how hay, which was a matter of life and death for Seth Hubbell's cattle, has become a minor source of nutrients for Doug Nelson's cows. While the harvesting of grass forage will continue to be important to Vermont dairy farmers, the harvesting of grass in its dry form, as hay, appears to be on the decline.

The Woodchuck Hunt
Drawn and illustrated for the
American Agriculturist.

Appendix

Letter of Marshall Carpenter to his grandchildren (Edward, Harry, Eunice, Frank, children of Henry Deming Carpenter and Eliza Steele Carpenter in Hope, North Dakota)

Derby, August 21, 1882

My Dear Grand Children.

It is so long since I have written a family letter that I hardly know where to begin. First of all I have to acknowledge the receipt of a letter from Frank a long time since which I have not answered, not because I did not appreciate it, and was more than pleased to receive it, but kept promising within myself I would write and often regretted my neglect but one thing after another transpired to hinder, and besides which I was sick and unable to do the chores after you and your father and Eddy left our and your old home. I did not go to the Barn but twice in two weeks or until Mr. Hinman moved here. I have been quite well since about the middle of March, since which time I had no leisure days, not even time to make our Garden. I have been engaged in the Holt estate as Commissioner over forty days, and have just closed and returned our papers to the Probate Court, and have found in favor of Mr. Spear 943.$. which will reduce his mortgage to Holt's Estate to about six hundred dollars, and the prospect is that neither party will take an appeal. I have also been Lister, and besides going through the town in April to take the usual or annual list, we have also in June been all through the town and appraising the whole real estate, I have made both Lists. Besides this I am one of the Appraisers and Commissioners in the Estates of Timothy Mitchell, Job C. Jenne, Revd. A Norcrop and Mrs. Hall, Mrs. John Grays *mother, so you will see that I have been tolerably busy. So much so that I have not even made a flower bed for Grandmother. Our garden this year looks more like the garden of the sluggard than otherwise. Now dear Children do not think that in the multitude of business I have been forgetful of you, no, no, not so; not a day nor scarce a single hour passes but something brings to mind some of you and then by association all of you, I do not see your father, Frankie and Eddie in the field, Harry about the house, or Eunice about her work &c. as in days gone by. To say that we are lonesome falls far short of properly expressing what our feelings are. You can never know how much pleasure a letter from Dakota gives us, And it is quite surprising to me that Grandmother is so ready to write in answer to your letters. Had it not been for that I should have written before, but she has kept you pretty well posted in matters at Derby. One thing has afforded us, and indeed all your friends in town a very great pleasure, and that is that you and Frank have, both given your hearts to Christ, a very important step indeed; and one that will afford you more happiness in this life than anything and all else besides. Now my dear Children, make it your first business to serve God, let his service be first and last every day. Make it a matter of every day work, and God will bless you abundantly, Nothing can so well prepare you for the business of life, and make you a blessing to your parents, to the community to yourselves as the religion of Jesus, and certainly nothing can enable you bear the ills and trials, and disappointments of life (for such things in the Providence of God will come,) as pure religious lives. And may you so live should you live even to old age so that you may look back upon lives spent in the service of your Lord and master. Oh never do as I have done, No never, but live agreeably to your profession. Remember that prayer is the life of the Christian, never neglect that duty. No person ever became a backslider on his knees.—I have very little to write that will be news as I learn yourselves and friends here keep up an active correspondence, so you are probably quite well posted, with what you get from Campes Paper, which I presume is quite interesting to you. Carrie Bates is quite sick and being naturally so feeble, does not stand a very good chance for recovery. A telegram from St. Pauls yesterday to Mrs. Job Jenne says Mr. Hunt is dead.— John F. Morrill is improving slowly and may recover. Betsey Orcutt is quite feeble, and appears to be running down. She may recover, but the probabilities are quite against such a result.—Now I wish to thank Eunice for her kind letter recd. last Saturday evening. Please remember me again, for it is a great pleasure to receive at our lonesome home a letter addressed to "Grandfather." I say "lonesome home," it is so, notwithstanding we have one of the best, and quietest familys, with us in the world, for they are truly very excellent people but it is not as it was with our own children and childrens children, but under the circumstances I do not think we could do better. I must tell Eddie what fine trappers Mr. Hinmans boys are. In the Spring we found woodchuck holes quite plenty in the mowing, so I told the boys I would give them five cents each for all they would catch. Up on Haying they had caught fifteen and thought they were pretty well cleaned out, So I raised the price to ten cents for old ones and five cents for cubs. They have now caught in the whole about twenty-five. You do not know how I want to see you all. I am reminded of you every day when about home, for I can scarce go anywhere about the buildings without seeing something to remind me of you. Yesterday while cleaning up and putting things in place in the shop I saw Franks lumber which was got out for Honey Boxes, and his Glass and I also came across Eddies old fife, and Harrys old wheelbarrow, also the little kettle that Aunt Phebe gave to Eunice, also the sleds you used to slide down the hills upon, and one of the scooters Eddie made last winter. When I go into the back chamber that I see the Old Desk Eddie used to keep his patterns and Fret saws in, and the first I know my eyes fill with tears, and I wonder if I shall ever see you again. And these small things you think so little of I prize as keepsakes. And by the way, I keep Frankies lumber and glass just where he kept it, and do not use it for any purpose. We have no Grandchildren now to play in the yard or under the shade of our trees, or pluck flowers from our garden. So it is, and cannot be helped. It may all be for the best and my earnest prayer is, that you all may realize all you have anticipated, and if so, I shall try and be content for I wish the greatest good to you all.— Perhaps you would be interested in matters that pertain to the farm so I will tell you something about that. The winter was probably the hardest one for the grass crop of any for many years. Our repeated snows, thaws and bare ground killed almost the whole of the clover of every variety, the Red, Alsike and White all went together. We had no clover on the farm this year except on the hill where we raised Oats and Rye last year, and that was greatly injured. There is no white clover growing this year, I do not think I have seen a hundred blossoms this year in highway or pasture. The piece of Red Clover that grew North West of the barn last year where we mowed the second crop, and fed it to the cows was clean Herds Grass this year, not a stalk of any kind of clover to be found on it, and so with every piece of grass upon the farm except the first piece spoken of. The spring was very cold and backward, and up to past the middle of June it seemed that our Hay crop would be a failure. But after the weather became warmer grass began to grow and thicken up, and when it was fit to cut it was the handsomest crop of grass I ever saw standing. It was thick and remarkably tall and free from weeds. I think it is the biggest and best crop of hay I have ever seen where the land was in good condition, but upon poor lands like Saml Attlings, John F. Morrills, Emera Stewarts, and George Eatons the poorest I have ever seen, taken as a whole I think it much more than average. Our barns were never so full before, I think cer-*

tainly three or four tons more than last year. The cold moist spring although farmers were complaining and predicting a failure of all crops, I think the cold backward spring was our salvation, for it kept the crops from growing except by getting thoroughly rooted, and the roots well spred; whereas, if it had been dry and warm, the grass would have grown in stalks instead of root, and instead of a broad setting, would have thrown up a stalk or two for seed only. Our Oat crop is of very heavy growth, and bids fair to equal that of last year. Barley a very fair but not remarkably heavy crop. Our wheat we think extra good. Corn light, and late, will require a week or ten days to get it fairly in the milk. We prepared the ground well and phosphated as usual. The wire worms have worked upon it quite as bad as they did last year. We planted the most of it with Beans between the hills. It has been the general complaint, that the worms were eating corn badly. Taking it all in all corn is doubtless a failure, so far as I can learn all through Northern Vermont, at least east of the Green Mountains and in Canada. Potatoes are looking finely but are quite late, tops are fresh and green, and no appearance of rust yet. Tubers of the Early Rose and other early varieties are of fair size and beginning to cook dry and break open in boiling. On account of the high prices last Spring large fields were planted. As is usual on the farm the Turnip crop bids fair now to be large. Beans and Peas are late. Peas just hardening and Beans half grown in the pod. Apples an almost entire failure, this is emphatically the off year with them. All small fruits and berries scarce and poor. Strawberries some, Raspberries next to none. Our Pumpkins and Squash just in blossom, will require much good warm weather to ripen them.

Now after telling you about the crops, I will tell you where they are so you can see something how the farm looks. We have two acres of Corn and one half acre of Turnips growing on the flat East of the house; the corn on the East side, next the wall, extending from the road, north to *the foot of the hill. The Turnips also on the north side of the road betwen the corn and the Shade trees, and also extending to the foot of the hill and west to within about fourteen feet of the Trees and to within about Six feet of the Ice House and the Shop door. The South side of the road from the gate to the Garden is planted to Peas nearest the Gate (about Six or Eight rods) and all the rest to Beans. Our potatoes, two acres, are planted on the hill north of the barn extending East to a line from the Shop to the Pasture bars that open into Hardscrabble Pasture. The long rows extend as far west as the NorthWest corner of the barn, West of which is our fodder corn, 1/4 acre, which extends West to the Clover piece and North to the apple tree stump in the East End of the old nursery—back of the fodder corn, and on the west of the long rows of potatoes, say six or eight rods down onto the flat NorthWest of the old nursery, and over north to the pasture fence. We have Wheat on all the Corn ground of last year except a strip of half an acre on the South side down next the swail west of the Spring— which by the way (that is the spring) is an entire failure. The Rain has not run but two days since we put down the new water tank last fall. We have Barley and Turnips on the piece of old mowing west of the Corn ground of last year, and between that and last years wheat ground and extending north to where we raised Turnips two years ago, down by the Maples where Old John was buried,— and on the piece between the Turnip ground and our Potatoes this year we have Rye & Oats. And where we raised Potatoes last year we have Rye and Oats, and a very heavy crop.—Grandmother wrote you some time since about calves and Lambs. Our Calves are very good. I think they are very promising. They are speckled some Red and White. We have not sold our Lambs or Wool yet, Have been offered but $3.25 for our male Lambs, the Ewes we shall keep. In July we were offered 23 cts for wool, we can get but 21 or 2 for it now. Shall probably hold it till next season, Mr. Hinman likes the Cows very well, they have had* *plenty of feed this summer, and are in good flesh. The Brindle two year old proves first best, the blind one did not have a Calf, but is growing finely this summer. The Red and White three year old will not make a very good cow. The Black and White one Mr. Hinman calls the best cow in the lot of her age. The Black one will make a fair cow, say about middling—Maria is dry this summer, girts a little over six feet and is good beef and is for sale. Our yearlings are very good ones except the small one, the calf of the Red Ayershire cow. She is as handsome as any one of them but is very small. "Old Gray" is in very good flesh and travels better than she did last year. She has been worked the past spring quite a good deal on the Harrow and has done the Tedding and raking this summer and has been driven to mill and of errands more or less all summer, and has run in the pasture since about the middle of June. Old Sally is as fat and lazy as ever, Slick as a Seal and as fat as pork.—The horse bought of Newmare just the morning you left Derby proves to be a very good one. Always ready to eat and drink and as ready to his part of the work, but is too quick for Sally and does more than his share of the work.—The Pigs we bought of Mr. Thatcher last fall do not prove very good ones. We have fed them well but they will not weigh as much by 75 to 100 lbs. as ours did last year. Now I have told you a long story, and mostly about affairs of the farm hoping you will all be interested. Kiss Harry for Grandmother and for me, and tell him something of us, and of the farm so that he may retain something in his memory of his babyhood home, notwithstanding I cannot be reconciled to your being so far away, I rejoice in your successes and bright prospects, and if I never meet you more on Earth, hope to meet you all in heaven. Thanks for the many letters you have written. A letter from any of you is always joyfully received. Love to all—Write often. Believe one whom I subscribe myself your affectionate Grandfather M. Carpenter.*

"New England Storm, Newbury, Vermont"

Wood engraving by Hiram Campbell Merrill, 1945.
Courtesy of Vermont Historical Society.

Notes

Preface

[1]Hinton Rowan Helper, *The Impending Crisis of the South: How to Meet It.* (New York: A. B. Burdick, 1860), 50-53.

Chapter 1

[1]Seth Hubbell, *A Narrative of the Sufferings of Seth Hubbell & Family, in His Begginning a Settlement in the Town of Wolcott, in the State of Vermont* (Danville, Vt.: Ebenezer Eaton, 1824; reprint, Bennington, Vt.: Vermont Heritage Press; Hyde Park, Vt.: Vermont Council on the Humanities and Public Issues, 1986), 2-3.

[2]Ibid., 5.

[3]Thomas Hutchinson, *The History of Massachusetts from the First Settlement Thereof in 1628, Until the Year 1750,* Vol. I, 3rd ed. (Salem: Thomas C. Cushing, 1795), 427; Ulysses Prentiss Hedrick, *A History of Agriculture in the State of New York* (New York: New York State Agricultural Society, 1933; reprint, New York: Hill and Wang, 1966), 343; Samuel Pettengill, *The Yankee Pioneers: A Saga of Courage* (Rutland, Vt.: Charles E. Tuttle, 1971), 45.

[4]John Burroughs, *Signs and Seasons*, vol. 7 of *The Writings of John Burroughs* (Boston: Houghton Mifflin, 1886), 251.

Chapter 2

[1]Town of Essex, *Land Records*, Books 1-4.

[2]Information on the Castle farm, crops, and activities for 1831 comes from Marshall Castle's diary, Marshall Castle Papers, Box 1, Folder 138, Wilbur Collection, Bailey/Howe Library, University of Vermont. An event that is dated in the text has an entry on that date in the diary and will not be further footnoted.

[3]The daily wages were calculated by dividing the number of days George Bicknal worked into the wages he received. This

wage is below the daily average of sixty-two cents and above the monthly average for 1831 of nine dollars with board as indicated in Thurston Adams, *Prices Paid by Vermont Farmers for Goods and Services and Received by Them for Farm Products, 1790-1940, Wages of Vermont Farm Labor 1780-1940* (Burlington, Vt.: Vermont Agricultural Extension Service, 1944), 90.

[4]Fred E. Crawford, *The Life and Times of Oramel Crawford: Vermont Farmer 1809-1888* (privately printed, 1952), 201.

[5]June 30 is the earliest Marshall Castle started haying, according to his diary. The average starting date was July 11.

[6]David Tresemer, *The Scythe Book* (Brattleboro, Vt.: By Hand and Foot, Ltd., 1981), 62.

[7]Crawford, 100; Tresemer, 52.

[8]Jared Van Wagenen, Jr., *The Golden Age of Homespun* (New York: Hill and Wang, 1963), 235.

[9]Walter Needham and Barrows Mussey, *A Book of Country Things* (Brattleboro, Vt.: Stephen Greene Press, 1965), 25. Needham states that a hand mower cut an eight-foot swath.

[10]Ibid., 62.

[11]Tresemer, 55; Crawford, 42; Samuel Deane, *The New England Farmer or Georgical Dictionary* (Worcester, Mass.: Press of Isaiah Thomas, 1792), 148. The author used Deane's suggestions for haymaking as the basis for the haying sequence described in this chapter.

[12]Donald Kilborn, Sr., interview with author, Derby, Vt., 27 January 1982, 2, 20; Miss Elaine Anderson, interview with author, Newport, Vt., 12 April 1982, 8. Typescripts of the taped interviews of Donald Kilborn, Sr., and Elaine Anderson are in the possession of the author. Page numbers refer to these typescripts.

[13]The description of yoking the oxen is based on a demonstration seen at the Farmers' Museum, Cooperstown, New York, in June 1971.

[14]Eric Sloane, *The Seasons of America Past* (New York: Funk and Wagnalls, 1972), 70-71; Kilborn, Sr., typescript, 12-13.

Chapter 3

[1]Printed material on the life of Marshall Carpenter's son in the Dakota Territory was acquired from Mrs. Arlene Vogel of Bozeman, Montana, Carpenter's great-great-granddaughter; United States Bureau of Census, *Tenth Census of the United States 1880; Population Schedules—Vermont* (Washington, D.C.: Bureau of Census, 1880).

[2]U.S. Bureau of Census, *State of Vermont 1880 Agricultural Census* (Washington, D.C.: Bureau of Census, 1880), 11.

[3]Marshall Carpenter letter to his grandchildren, 21 August 1882, 5. Photocopy acquired from Mrs. Arlene Vogel of Bozeman, Montana, is in the manuscript collection of the Vermont Historical Society (see appendix).

[4]Carpenter letter, 6.

[5]Carpenter letter gives the names of two of the horses, Old Sally and Old Gray. It refers to a third as the "Newmare horse." Information on harnessing and hitching horses provided by Stanley Wilson interview with author, Derby, Vt., 12 April 1982, 54-59. Typescripts of the taped interviews with Stanley Wilson are in the possession of the author. Richard Bacon, "Working with a Draft Horse," *The Forgotten Arts: Book Three* (Dublin, N.H.: Yankee, Inc., 1976), 52-56.

[6]Wilson typescript, 17.

[7]Kilborn, Sr., typescript, 14.

[8]Anderson typescript, 15.

[9]Charles W. Dickerman and Charles L. Flint, eds., *How To Make the Farm Pay; or, the farmer's book of practical information on agriculture, stock raising, fruit culture, special crops, domestic economy & family medicine* (Philadelphia: Zeigler & McCurdy, 1871), 121; Anderson typescript, 5-8, 10.

[10]Wilson typescript, 11.

[11]Ibid.; Carpenter letter, 10.

[12]Silas Houghton interview with author, Derby, Vt., 6 January 1982.

[13]Wilson typescript, 11.

[14]Ibid., 8-9.

[15]Carpenter letter, 6.; *1880 Agricultural Census.*

Chapter 4

[1]*Orleans County Monitor*, 8 August 1923, 7.

[2]Town of Derby, *Town Records: Book 17*, 130-131.; William Jeffrey, *Successful Vermonters: A Modern Gazetteer of Caledonia, Essex, and Orleans Counties* (East Burke, Vt.: Historical Publishing Co., 1904), 237.

[3]Mrs. Ethel Rowell interview with author, Derby, Vt., 12 July 1982 (not taped); Kenneth Rowell interview with author, Derby, Vt., 19 July 1982 (taped and transcribed).

[4]Town of Derby, *Town Records: Book 41*, 110; Kenneth Rowell typescript.

[5]Kilborn, Sr., typescript, 9.

[6]John Deere Company, *The Operation, Care and Repair of Farm Machinery*, 16th ed. (Moline, Ill.: John Deere Co., n.d.), 182. Hereafter referred to as *Operation*.

[7]Wilson typescript, 15.

[8]Kenneth Rowell typescript, 4.

[9]*Operation*, 186.

[10]Wilson typescript, 43-44.

Chapter 5

[1]Particulars of the farming of Don Kilborn, Jr., were reconstructed from interviews with Donald Kilborn, Jr., in Derby, Vt., 20, 23, and 24 July, 1982. These interviews were not taped, but the author has notes.

[2]Robert Bancroft, "Machinery Components (24)" (Burlington: University of Vermont, 1982). Computer program on the costs and capacities of agricultural equipment; Donald Kilborn, Jr., 20 July 1982.

[3]Kilborn, Jr., 20 July 1982.

[4]Ibid., 23 July 1982.

[5]Bancroft, 1.

[6]Calculated from Bancroft's tables, 1.

Chapter 6

[1]Don Kilborn, Jr., interview with author, Derby, Vt., May 1990.

[2]*United States Census of Agriculture, 1930: Vol. II, Reports by*

States with Statistics for Counties, and a Summary for the United States: Pt. 1 The Northern States. (Washington, D.C.: GPO, 1932), 170, 179.; *United States Census of Agriculture, 1987 Volume 1, Geographic Area Series:* Pt. 45 *Vermont: State & County Data (AC 87-A-45)* (Washington, D.C.: GPO, 1989); Neil Pelsue, telephone interview with author 23 October 1990. (Pelsue is a member of the Agriculture Economics Department of the University of Vermont in Burlington, Vermont.) The percentages and ratios were calculated by the author from information obtained from the preceding sources.

[3]Douglas Nelson interview with author, Derby, Vt., 26 May, 1990.

Glossary

Breeching. Part of the harness that goes on the horse's haunches, to prevent the collar from coming off as the horse backs.

Cock. 1. *n:* Small conical pile of hay that sheds the rain during the curing process; 2. *v:* To put hay into a pile or cock.

Conditioner. Tractor-powered machine, which consists of two horizontal rollers through which the cut grass is squeezed to crush the stalks to speed drying.

Cutter bar. Part of the mowing machine that does the actual mowing, consisting of a stationary bar with guards and the reciprocating section knives.

Forage. Fodder, chopped vegetation used as feed for domestic herbivores.

Freestall. Type of barn where the cattle are not tied, but allowed to move about freely. There may be stalls in which they can lie when resting.

Gad. A goad, a long slender stick with a leather strap on the end.

Gelding. Castrated male horse.

Guard. Part of a cutter bar, it protects the moving section from damage and contains stationary knives across which the moving section passes to cut the stalks of grain.

Hames. Two wood or metal curved bars fitted into the draft horse collar; secures the harness to the collar.

Haybine. Machine that combines the elements of a mower and a conditioner.

High drive. Ramp or bridge that leads to an upper level in a barn.

Kicker. Piece of equipment attached to the rear of a baler; throws the bales into a trailing wagon

Mow. 1. (mō) *v:* To cut grass with a scythe or machine; 2. (mau) *n:* Place in a barn for the storage of hay; *v:* To stow hay in a barn.

Neck yoke. Horizontal bar attached to the collar in front of each horse in a team and the pole of the wagon; holds back the wagon as the horses slow or back.

Nibs. Small handles on a snath.

Pitching on. Lifting a forkful of hay from the ground to the wagon.

Pitman. Wooden shaft that transfers the rotary motion of the mower flywheel to the reciprocating action of the section.

Round. Tier of tumbles on a hay wagon.

Scatterings. Scraps of hay left on the field after the hay has been picked up.

Section. 1. Part of the mowing machine that reciprocates to do the cutting; a narrow, flat steel bar to which are riveted triangular knives; 2. The triangular knife itself.

Silage. Green fodder preserved by fermentation in a silo.

Snath. Handle of a scythe; also called a snid or sneath.

Staddle. Frame upon which hay is stacked in the field; also called stackyard or stathel.

Swath. Path cut by a single pass of a mower.

Switchel. Non-alcoholic beverage used at haying time, made of vinegar, sweetener, ground ginger, and cold water.

Ted. To scatter mown hay so that it will dry faster.

Traces. Leather straps that transfer the force from a horse harness to the object being pulled.

Tumble. 1. *v:* To fold a segment of a windrow into a bundle to be picked up with a pitchfork; 2. *n:* The resulting bundle.

Weigh jar. Graduated glass jar that is part of the equipment in a milking parlor. It measures the quantity of milk a cow gives.

Whet. To sharpen by rubbing.

Whiffletree. Horizontal bar behind a horse to which the traces are attached.

Windrow. Long, narrow pile of hay raked together.